Twenty-eight years
Of
Grief

How Long Do We Choose To Carry The Burden??

By Wanda Nance

Dedicated

I want to dedicate this book to the loving memory of my mom. Twenty-three years she carried this consuming grief to her grave. You see a picture with a beautiful smile but I can see all the pain in her eyes, because I lived it with her.

Introduction

The story in this book is real life. Some of us have to face death so many times in our lives, and each person handles it in a different way. We all have heard the statement you're never supposed to out live your children. My mom did, not once, but twice and six months to the day apart, she lost both of her boys, my brothers. I was only sixteen. I thought that was terrible till God started impressing this book in my spirit. I started realizing just how young my mom was; she was only thirty-nine, and I was thirty-nine when I lost her. I think we always look at our parents as old but now I look back and see just how young she was carrying such a burden.

God never wants us to keep this grief. It is a choice we have to make. It is just like salvation. He wants us to choose life so we will spend eternal life with Him and each other.

So Moses the servant of the Lord died there in the land of Moab, according to the word of the Lord. Deuteronomy 34:5

Moses died and God instructed the children of Israel to go and mourn and gave them a time frame.

And the children of Israel wept for Moses in the plains of Moab thirty days. So the days of weeping and mourning for Moses ended.
Deuteronomy 34:8

As I write this book, my prayer is to pull out God's word and show you how God gives us time to mourn, but Satan wants to place a strong hold of grief on us, until it totally consumes our lives.
When that is all you think about. It eats you inside out. I've watched it; I've lived it! Twenty-three years my mom died with that strong hold. Another seven years from her death I carried it, and another three years God has been stirring this book in my spirit.
My prayer is for your healing of any

strong hold. Jesus has already taken care of it at the cross, but we have to choose to let them go. **It's okay to let them go!!!**

Remember good times and move on. Don't dwell on the sadness, the grief, or the bad times. I remember my family the front cover is a picture of my family.

All have passed away, my Mom was the last one and she died March 5, 2002. My dad passed away three years after my brothers on November 25, 1983.

I wanted to share a picture of my mom, my brother's and I we were so close even after we got older. I would go on dates with my oldest brother (Delbert). When Winfred bought his last car, he wanted me to go with him.

Delbert took care of us after Dad left because my Mom was working two jobs. Many times I look back and wonder how she made it. She was so strong she was my hero.

He did most of the cooking and we all cleaned. We all pulled together and did what we had to.

Two and half years before my brothers got killed.
We were celebrating my grandparents fifty
anniversary Harvey and Myrtle Shaw.

February 4, 2009 4:30 a.m. I awoke bursting into tears just out of nowhere. Then I remembered the moment in my life that stole my life of childhood and happiness all together. So I quickly asked God to heal me from this strong hold that had stolen my life. I lay there and began to think just this week God has brought death up to me to say a word of encouragement to someone else. So as I began to pray and have my quiet time with God, He said again twenty-eight years of grief. How long do you choose to carry it? No longer… It's been far too long. I let a great part of me die when my brothers were killed. I felt that we are supposed to miss them and think about them every day or we don't love them. I thought I should go to the graves over and over again. I think if I could just see them one minute I would feel so much better. All these thoughts would race through my mind at such a vulnerable age of sixteen when life was supposed to be good. I would drive down the road and imagine what I would do if I could see them just standing beside the road. I could read peoples' mind at first they didn't know what to say or not to say. After a while nobody said anything, and it was still a great loss for me every day.

I was hurting, confused and angry. Satan was having a field day with my mind and my emotions.

I didn't know God! He was there just waiting for me to call out to Him. But I never did. I didn't understand or even know how. I thought this was just a part of life. Nobody took the time to introduce me to a God who really cares, who heals, who delivers, our Father, our Creator. There were Christians all around me. I think back now and wonder why they didn't try was they scared that I would be mean? They didn't know what to say or how to say it. The truth I'm sure I would have been. Was it just not my time, or what? Why do some go through so much and never understand the Power of God and the peace that He can give? Is it to help someone else? I believe it is! It's hard to tell directions to a place that you have never been. But if you have been there time and time again you can tell someone else just how to get there and the short cut to take. Just fall on your knees! I've been there time and time again with grief. We think, so what; everybody goes through death and we do. But before I was an adult I had been to so many funerals. I remember people saying it comes in threes meaning that three people on one side of my family or the other were going to die. That was spoken in our family for several years. Was that a curse? It surely wasn't a blessing that they were speaking over me. Sometimes we are unaware of the danger that we put forth out of our mouth.

Today in our Sunday school class the teacher asked if you ever got mad at God and asked why? I thought long and hard as everybody voiced their opinions. I can't understand someone getting mad at God. I do remember lying in bed (when Winfred, my brother got killed) and asking God why him, why not me. He was always sick and I felt as if Mom really loved him more because of him being sick a lot. He was a happy- go-lucky guy always wanting to have fun. I couldn't bear feeling the pain I was feeling and in my own child like ways I thought my mom would not hurt as bad if it had been me. So I would lie there for several nights crying and saying the same thing over and over in my mind. But I truly don't remember getting mad at anyone, not even his friend who was driving. I do recall doubting, wondering and asking why and even what if... What really happened? In accidents you never know for sure what happens! It is harder to accept and let go, when there are so many questions running through your mind. That brings up years of bitterness. But to get mad or blame God I didn't understand or I don't even understand that mindset today! But that's me. Of course there were several in the class who had got mad at God and that was okay too. Think it was a surprise to God? Today I just trust God with my heart, soul and life. If things don't turn out my way it's not because He doesn't love me or want the best for me. The Bible says it rains on the just and unjust. I know He has plans for me to prosper and to be in good health, and He is with me always even to the end of the earth. So I may not understand the things I go through, but I do understand that it is to bring glory to Him. Even the tragedies in our life He can turn evil into good. Just hold on to the hem of His garment. He will never leave us or forsake us. I can say this because I have felt the pain of losing several loved ones while lost in this dying world. Then the peace of Him carries me through the pain of losing loved ones. My heart goes out to the lost people going through times of not understanding and wanting to know why, and needing someone to take the pain, just someone to truly care. Believe me they can't understand the love and peace of Christ. A Christian can't understand the pain they are going through. (Don't even try just show love you can't take the pain or understand their pain.)

Sometimes we are so quick to judge or to say things like "Was he saved? Did they know Christ?" We as humans don't know

Anyone's heart yes, the Bible says we can tell by the fruit they bear and it also says not to judge unless you want the same measure judged unto you. But I never understood getting mad at God. I never really knew God and trusted Him to be my all. I never prayed asking and believing that He is the answer to all things. I just remember at these times in my life crying out and asking why and why not me. Then six months to the night later my oldest brother was killed. This time more questions ran through my mind, but I was scared to ask thinking it was my fault because I had questioned God. You didn't do that! I was scared He would take my mom and she's all I had left. I feared God. I didn't know Him, I feared Him. Thinking He was this great big God ready to punish you if you did wrong. That is so far from the truth. He is this great big God who knows your every thought, but He loves you unconditionally without you doing anything. He loved us first and sent His son to die for us to have life with Him, not to punish us His is a love closer than a brother, parent or even a child. So I just buried all the pain inside wondering if it was my fault but not asking. I was too scared. The devil can plant some crazy thoughts in your mind and pain that is unthinkable. I carried this pain and tried my best to carry my mom's for the next twenty-three years she lived. I never wanted her to hurt anymore. But little did I know that a lot of my choices in life would have so much grief on her. I never stopped to think that way, when I moved away to Texas and the pain of me being gone. I would call her every day but only get to see her every few months. Then years later in 2002 when I had a major car wreck that should have taken my life. I was in so much pain but refused to shed a tear because I could see all the pain I had put my mom in again. I knew the pain I was feeling and I could not imagine the pain she was feeling. I never try to imagine the pain or feel someone else's feeling because I know that is impossible. All people handle pain differently. Some are closer than others. Some have to deal with the pain of losing them and the pain of their relationship at the time of their death. God made each one of us different so why do we think we handle pain the same. Just love them and have compassion with them as Jesus did. If they laugh, laugh with them, if they cry, cry with them, if they talk, listen… That is the greatest witness that you could be to them. Then when the Holy Spirit opens the door it will be right. It will be of God and not of man! I go back to the book of Ruth. Do you think Naomi was angry with God? I think she was. After she had lost her husband and both sons she decided to return to the land of Judah her people. But when she got there in verse twenty she said:

And she said unto them, call me not Naomi (pleasant), call me Mara (bitter): for the Almighty hath dealt very bitterly with me. I went out full, and the Lord hath brought me home again empty: why then call ye me Naomi, seeing the Lord hath testified against me, and the Almighty hath afflicted me? So Naomi returned, and Ruth the Moabites, her daughter-in-law, with her, which returned out of the country of Moab: and they came to Bethlehem in the beginning of barley harvest.

Ruth 1: 20-22

As we read the scriptures we can see she was very bitter with God and she blamed Him for the loss of her husband and sons. She states, "I went away full but the Lord has brought me home empty." I would say that was pointing her finger at God. How many times as a country and individual have you heard why didn't or did God allow that to happen? We so easily point our finger at God. The Bible states that we will reap what we sow. Not maybe or maybe a crop failure, but if you plant corn, corn is coming up not watermelons. We so easily want to blame someone else for our crop when harvest comes; and God seems to be the easy one. He created everything so why not Him? He could have stopped it from happening. When all along it's not God's fault that bad things happen, His word says we can walk in blessings or curses. We have to line up our life and follow Him to walk in blessings. Do bad things happen then? Yes, they can because God allows it to for a reason out of our understanding. His word says that our ways are not His ways, and our understanding is not His understanding. When we were a child we walked like a child and talked like a child but as we grow in Christ we put away childish ways. We understand that sometimes we don't understand.

Naomi had lost everything- her husband and her two sons and she was thinking it was because they had moved into the land Moab. First her husband died and then her sons married two Moabites women and her sons died. Do you think that's one reason she wanted both daughters-in-law to go back to their parents because she was afraid that she would not be walking in God's will if they went with her? She had already lost everything; she so desperately wanted to get back in God's will to her people. She was angry, frustrated, desperate and withdrawn. But Ruth was not going back. She was staying with Naomi no matter what. Where she died she would die. That was devoted, a pure heart going into a strange land with different people. That would be like an American going into a totally different nation. She had sold out and God saw her pure heart and she found favor with Boaz. She asked Naomi if she could work the field and pick what was left over after it was harvested. And at first Boaz found favor with her and told his men to leave extra for her and not to bother her. When she went back and told Naomi who she had found favor, Naomi's mind started clicking, well, well, well. And the story ends with Naomi getting back in the path of God's will. Boaz and Ruth married and their son is the grandfather of King David who is an ancestor of Jesus Christ. God knows all things and from our tragedies can come blessings if we will follow God and not ourselves. We must allow God to heal that sorrow and not turn it into bitterness. Satan likes nothing better than to give us a spirit of Grief. Yes I said it. It is a strong hold that you have allowed to attach to you. I had for years! Like

Ruth He will call you into the unknown. We just have to be willing to go and trust Him. Ruth had lost her husband but she didn't know God as Naomi did so she didn't blame Him. She had nothing but trust and faith in the great I am. She had true sorrow for her mother-in-law, took care of her and forgot about feeling sorrow for herself.

Isn't that what we do? We feel if we don't think about those loved ones every day and the tragedy of losing them, we might just forget about them. That is so far from the truth. We don't have to make ourselves miserable as grieving to show that we loved them. The best way is to allow God to come into our hearts and bring peace, true peace and understanding that we are not in control. When that person comes to your mind, think and talk about the good times and move on and don't linger on it. As God told Israel when Moses died to mourn for thirty days and then move on. There is a lot in that scripture that we need to understand. After a while that mourning turns into grief, bitterness, and anger that is a spirit that has attached to you to control your every thought and direction of each and every day for years if you so allow Satan to take control of your life.

But to realize it we just think we are missing our loved one. No, it has taken possession of your life and you are no longer you.

Just like anger His word tells us not to let the sun go down without forgiving the one you are angry at. Anger has such a fast strong hold on us and turns into bitterness. God doesn't tell us this to hurt us. He tells us this so Satan won't have a strong hold on us. Satan wants to kill, steal, and destroy!

In Genesis 50 when Joseph's father Israel died. Joseph fell on his father's face and wept over him. He was embalmed which took forty days, and then they mourned for seventy days before Joseph took his father to his grave. He had requested to be buried by his father, Joseph's grandfather. When they got to the gravesite they mourned another seven days. Then they returned to Egypt.

So with Moses they mourned thirty days and with Israel they mourned one hundred and seventeen days. But the two stories are they went back to their lives. They moved on they didn't forget them but they moved on with their lives.

Many times I think God wants us to have the heart of a child so we can see and hear what He is telling us. My son,

Austin, was six when my mom passed away. I recall when we went in to view mother's body first. Austin walked up to the casket and shortly he left. He went to the break room and drew what he saw. He had to see this because he didn't know the spirit left the body. As you see he had drawn her body still in the casket. But as he seen her spirit above and only in the spirit, they could have told each other I love you. It still touches me today to see his drawing, and I hope it really helps you. They love us but they are gone to the Father just like one day we will. If you know Jesus as your Lord and Savior

Austin Nance   03/06/2002

This week as I went to my uncle's funeral, before I left home I asked God what you want me to learn from this. I believe from every trial there is knowledge to learn if only we take the time to ask God to show us. I began to watch fellowship and ponder on the situation. I knew I wasn't quite finish with this book. As the funeral began I watched a very dear pastor preach the funeral with so much pain in him. Not necessarily this funeral but so many he had preached, the pain and the grief had become his enemy. I use that word because he stated it a couple times, death is our enemy. Death is our enemy we don't know how to deal with it or what to say to the other person. But as Jesus did He wept with them had compassion for them. Oh, He knew they were in a much better place, but He still showed compassion. As I left the funeral my heart broke for the pastor so many times we don't realize what a burden it is for that pastor to carry. They devote their lives to God and to serve people, they become attached part of their family. But they suppose to stand strong and have all this great wisdom when the truth is they are just human and they hurt just like us. But it hurt me so to see him so broken inside. He has carried a many burden and preached many funerals of his flock.

And a week before this I went to a dear friend of mine husband's funeral, which he showed me all faces of grief some of us paint on a smile, laugh and carry on with everybody and can't be still because we know if we did we would fall apart.

Others are very withdrawn will speak and be kind but please just go on and leave me alone, because you don't possibly know how I feel. Then there are those that truly know they have gone on to a better place and I will see them again today I maybe sorrowful but tomorrow I will rejoice of their homecoming. I will see them again!

I remember the day that grief had such a strong hold on me that I couldn't go to a funeral home or my family church without falling apart because there was so much pain hidden deep inside me. I recall the Sunday morning I was at my church when God spoke to me for me to go to my home church that night. Everything in me didn't want to go I asked a friend to go with me. As I walked in I fought the tears back and fellowship with the people there. When service began I raised my hand and began to praise the Lord I had already held back all the tears that I could. As I began to praise this burden was lifted off of me that night. I have been back to the church a few times since and I will always come into His courts with thanksgiving and praise. Since that journey I have even worked at a funeral home. I refuse to let Satan destroy me with grief. Will they be other funerals and painful events sure they will. That is life we are not promise a life without pain or grief. We are told that there will be trials and tribulations. We grow in wisdom and faith through life's trials.

Just as Job was a righteous man blameless and who feared God. God allowed Satan to do whatever he wanted but couldn't take his life. Satan did wipe out all that he had children, livestock, and servants and even struck him with boils all over his body. But Jobs reply was;

Then Job arose, tore his robe, and shaved his head; and he fell to the ground and worshiped. And he said:
"Naked I came from my mother's womb, and naked shall I return there. The Lord gave, and the Lord has taken away; Blessed be the name of the Lord."
In all this Job did not sin are charge God with wrong.

Job 1:20-22

As Job lost everything yet he still praised the Lord and God restored him. For such a long time I would read the end of Job and think yea but what about the children he lost. God gave him more but the pain and sorrow for the ones he lost that couldn't be replaced. When I wasn't seeing the full picture Job never lost them they had just gone on home. Job knew that one day they would all be together.

Job and King David both trusted in the Lord, Job never sinned where King David did but always was quick to repent. Both were in worship with the Lord when losing their children. Job worshipped and prayed after he heard the terrible news and King David prayed and fasted before his son die.

King David when God told him because of his sin that the child would die. He prayed and fasted before the Lord hoping that God would change His mind. But after the child died scripture says;

And he said, "While the child was alive, I fasted and wept; for I said, "Who can tell whether the Lord" will be gracious to me, that the child may live? "But now he is dead; why should I fast? Can I bring him back again? I shall go to him, but he shall not return to me."
2 Samuel 12:22, 23

That would be a heavy burden to bear to know that because of what you did that your child would die. But David understood God. The Bible states He was a man after God's own heart. He chased God; he prayed and sought His ways. David failed in many ways but he was quick to repeat and turn back to God's way. He knew he could not bring his son back, but he would see him again. Forever is not on this earth but forever is in heaven with God our Father, Jesus our Savior, and all of our love ones who have gone on before us.

This is where grief takes us and keeps us if we allow it for years, months, days for a life time. It's our choice!

As I finished this book, I began to deal with a whole different area in grief. Yes it had been in my spirit for several years. And I wrestled and cried with it to myself but did not bring it to the light. I kept it in the darkness of my spirit and soul. I was asked to speak at a women's conference this coming September. As I began to write this book, I knew this was what I was speaking on "Fear of Grief". But that grief began to go beyond death. Several years back one of my mentors Sandra Curtis came to me and laid her hand on my shoulder and began to speak in my life. "When you let go of everything and everybody, then God is going to move mightily in your life." I began to cry deep down in my spirit because then I knew that it was God, and I walking this journey alone… It has been several years since she spoke that over me but I remember it as if it was this moment. I knew it was coming down to a great sacrifice to walk out my destiny. My flesh doesn't want to be alone but my spirit longs for that time of me and God…

As I said He began to walk me through different areas of grief. This Mother's Day of 2012, we, my family was eating dinner enjoying the day after church when my life turned up side down. My son had begun to make some wrong decisions in his life, and they were worried about him. They had seen him the day before mud riding four-wheelers, and he was drinking and had turned the four-wheeler over on him three times. If it hadn't been for this girl and young kid he would have drowned because he was so drunk he couldn't get up, so I was told. As I waited to get all the facts before I said something to him, I began to pray and seek advice. I knew I had to do something. I began to talk to him that night and tell him that while he was under my roof, there would be no more hanging out with his friends that he could go to work and go to his sister's and come home. If he left he wouldn't be in his truck because it was still in my name till he turns eighteen. We had been down this road before, and if he hangs with them he is going to drink. So that following Tuesday we had a great day (started off a little distant.) We went to Jackson just to hang out, look at motorcycles, eat lunch and come back home. He told me he was glad I came down hard on him. That way he could save his money and accomplish his dreams. I was thinking, "Wow, thank you, Lord. I was praising God," when He had changed his mind totally by the next day and by the end of the week he had gotten an apartment and moved to Union where he worked. That was not what I had planned at all. He is only seventeen and he had one more year of school. I began to see everybody putting their kid's pictures on facebook of graduation and him telling me he is not going to finish. He will just get his GED and go on to college. When my heart is breaking because I have already walked that road, it's not so easy to keep a job go to college and pay your bills. He has so many dreams in his life that he wants to accomplish, and God has blessed him with such ability to fix things. When he was sixteen he took the motor out of a truck and replaced it by himself. God had built that in him. When he was young he would tinker on my old four-wheeler, and I would pray and the next thing I knew he would have it running. And at seventeen he is rebuilding engines at this small engine repair shop. I'm so proud of him in so many ways but my heart breaks to see where the enemy wants to take him and he can't see it, or doesn't want to. Because sin is fun for a season the Bible warns us of that.

He moved out that Friday night and that weekend I tried hard to paint on that smile and keep going. I did the best I could but when I was by myself all I could do was cry. My daughter told me, "Mom you never went on with your life; it's always been you and Austin." That was so true but I knew one day he would grow up and leave but not this way or at this age. That Sunday morning as I began to go out the door to church by myself I realized that he wasn't coming later. The Lord spoke and told me that he was my prodigal child. Now I see so deep into that story. I can feel the father's pain, longing and waiting for that son to return not just to him but to the Lord. Then when that son returned he was totally changed at heart. He had been eating with the pigs. He wanted the adventure of the world and asked for his inheritance and the father gave it to him. And he waited and looked each day for his return. As I began to read and study this story, I returned Austin's truck to him, and I am waiting for his return. Maybe not physically but spiritually he will return. The Bible says raise up a child the way he shall go and when he is old he shall not depart from it. Austin is not just my prodigal son. He is the reason that we started going to church when he was five. He was so persistent that we go and later that he gets baptized as Jesus was. He wouldn't give up; he wouldn't let it go till he was baptized. God is not finished with him yet He's just working out the details of his testimony. And I can walk around in grief or I can walk in grace and be about my Father's business. My heart has been for several years to open a home for women, and now it's time!!! I'm living in a three bedroom home that I can turn into a home for women. And I just want to see where God grows it to. I have nine acres for it to grow on. I am excited to see what God is going to do…. Devil; don't mess with me I'm not walking in your grief. I'm walking in God's grace!!!!

A lot has taken place in these last few months and I refuse to give Satan any glory from this area in our lives. The last few months I had prayed and asked others to pray that Austin would change his mind and finish home school so he would graduate. But our Father gives us the desires of our heart my heart was to see him walk with his high school class. Austin had wanted to go back to Sebastopol High School after about two months of home schooling. He finished out his eleventh grade home schooling. Monday, July 23, 2012, around 10:30 pm I had just got home from work when Austin text me wanting to go back to Sebastopol school. I told him we would see what we had to do if it was possible. I began to pray that night that God would make a way that He would open all the doors and make this possible. So the next morning I went to the school and talked with the councilor and told her what he wanted to do and if it was possible for him to graduate with his class. She told me what all we had to do and it was possible but would take a lot of hard work from Austin and he would have several tests to take. I text him and told him what she said and that evening he moved back home. Wednesday morning we both went back to the school with all the information and talked with Mrs. McKee again. She was very encouraging to him told him all the tests he had to take but if he passed by, Christmas he would be a senior and would get to graduate with his class. God is good!!!

That Friday night he went to the fair on his way home he got pulled over by the cops so he had his wallet out and wasn't aware that he had lost it until late Saturday afternoon. He came back to the house we search everywhere and then he started back tracking he found his wallet lying on the ground at a convenient store where all the kids hang out. It is the busiest store in town and his wallet was still lying on the ground and no one had touched it all his money was still there. God is good!!!

God has showed us just how faithful and loving He is but it's up to us to walk it out. Yes, the shelter is still open and Austin has to work hard to accomplish what he wants but God made it all possible.

But You have seen, for You observe trouble and grief, to repay it by Your hand. The helpless commits himself to You; You are the helper of the fatherless.
Psalm 10:14

As I began to finish this book the spirit began to wrestle with me in this area. I have also experience and watched it over and over again with my hands tied and my heart broken by it. The area the enemy can so attacks a child with grief a longing fatherless grief, where the father gives us charter of who we are. God word says, "He is the helper of the fatherless." So we have to trust and rest in His word and to realize we are special to Him. And He has us in the palm of His hand.

When my dad left us when I was nine years old, it didn't bother me as it did my brothers. I was glad because I knew that the fighting and the fear of him coming home drunk and the abuse would stop. But my brothers missed him our father. I never had that longing for him till we got the phone call he was dead, then it was all too late. The last time which was at my brother's funeral we had gotten into an argument because he had been drinking and saying awful things. He told me I would never see him alive again. Those were the last words that rung in my mind for years, when I would think about him.

As the years passed I have watched and seen this pain through my niece, my daughter, and my son. And even know my grandson ask questions to his mom about her dad that she can't answer.

My niece was only a year and half when my brother died. My daughter Amanda was five when her dad, Jerry died and my son Austin was fourteen when his dad Mike died. Leaving each one with so many questions running through their minds why, what if, if only, as they grew up fatherless not understanding the pain the grief of loneness. It is so hard especially with a child of no understanding just a great big world of pain, shut up inside and no way to get it out and so often overlooked by adults. Father's day, birthdays, Christmas while everyone celebrates you think what if he was here? Just seeing other kids with their dad's and not understanding what a roll that a dad plays in their life. Then it's preached over and over what a roll your dad plays in your life and you sit there hearing that and you have no dad. That is a lie from the devil he comes to kill, steal and destroy. God is your Father your earthly father maybe gone. But He left us with a promise that He is the Father to the fatherless. He will direct our path, He will give us charter, and He is always with us we are not less than we are greater than. He is the author and finisher of our faith. He is the healer, He is the deliverer, and He will restore your heart. We may not be able to see Him in person but we sure can feel Him with us every moment of every day if we will let Him into our hearts to stay. It's our choice! He promises:

A father of the fatherless, a defender of windows, is God in His holy habitation. God sets the solitary in families; He brings out those who are bound into prosperity; But the rebellious dwell in a dry land.
Psalm 68:5-6

Defend the poor and fatherless; Do justice to the afflicted and needy.
Psalm 82:3

*The Lord opens the eyes of the blind;
The Lord raises those who are bowed
down; The Lord loves the righteous, The
Lord watches over the strangers; He
relieves the fatherless and widow; But
the way of the wicked He turns upside
down.*

Psalm 146:8-9

Psalm 94 God the refuge of the righteous
as David writes over and over all through
Psalm crying out about the strangers,
widows and the fatherless. And these are
the ones that God commands us to take
care off.

*I will not leave you orphans; I will come
to you.*

John 14:18

Here are several scriptures that I hope will help you to walk out your grief into grace…

Have mercy on me, O Lord, for I am in trouble; My eyes wastes away with grief, Yes, my soul and my body!
For my life is spent with grief, and my years with sighing; My strength fails because of my iniquity, and my bones waste away.   Psalm 31:9, 10

You have turned for me my mourning into dancing; you have put off my sackcloth and clothed me with gladness.
Psalm 30:11

Remember your Creator before the silver cord is loosed, Or the golden bowl is broken, or the pitcher shattered at the fountain, or the wheel broken at the well. Then the dust will return to the earth as it was, and the spirit will return to God who gave it.

"Vanity of vanities," says the Preacher,
"All is vanity."

Ecclesiastes 12:6-8

Death, where is thy sting? O
grave, where is thy victory?

1 Corinthians 15:55

For as much then as the children are
partakers of flesh and blood, He also
Himself likewise took part of the same;
that through death He might destroy him
that had the power of death, that is, the
devil;
And deliver them who through fear of
death were all their lifetime subject to
bondage.

Hebrews 2:14, 15

But God will redeem my soul from the
power of the grave: for He shall receive
me.

Psalms 49:15

He will swallow up death in victory; and the Lord God will wipe away tears from off all faces.
                    Isaiah 25:8

That whosoever believeth in Him should not perish, but have eternal live.
                    John 3:15

For I am persuaded, that neither death, nor life, nor angels, nor principalities, nor powers, nor things present, nor things to come, nor height, nor depth, nor any other creature, shall be able to separate us from the love of God, which is in Christ Jesus our Lord.
                    Romans 8:38, 39

To everything there is a season,
A time for every purpose under heaven:
A time to be born,
And a time to die;
A time to plant,
And a time to pluck what is planted;
A time to kill,

And a time to heal;
A time to break down,
And a time to build up;
A time to weep,
And a time to laugh;
A time to mourn,
And a time to dance;
A time to cast away stones;
And a time to gather stones;
A time to embrace,
And a time to refrain from embracing;
A time to gain,
And a time to lose;
A time to keep,
And a time to throw away;
A time to tear,
And a time to sew;
A time to keep silence,
And a time to speak;
A time to love,
And a time to hate;
A time of war,
And a time of peace.

Ecclesiastes 3:1-8

After my mom's funeral the funeral home sent me these scriptures (Ecclesiastes 3:1-8).
Time and time again I would read them, and they brought such great comfort to me. I pray this book does that for you...
I wanted to share with you how my God blesses and restore what the canker worm eats up. These are a few pictures of my family. And even though we have our ups and downs God has blessed me with the most wonderful kids…

My beautiful two kids Amanda, Austin and myself.

Amanda my beautiful daughter and Brad the greatest Son-in-law that I could ever ask for.

We have all just walked the track for the kids preparing for some dirt bike racing. At that time Austin was racing four-wheelers and Zack and Prestin my grandchildren were racing dirt bikes. Great memories some days we have laughed, cried and rejoiced together.

Austin 022, and Zack 15 racing each other hard to watch both at one time.

Prestin 88 leading the race ☺

Braxtin our little man loves him some dirt bikes!

Alexis and her new race machine she has to keep up with the boys. She is a little out numbered but she holds her on.

Austin, Prestin, Braxtin, Alexis, and Zack. God has truly
blessed me with a beautiful healthy family.
"Children are blessings from God"

Thank you, for taking the time to read my
book. I pray that you are truly blessed and
set free of any strong holds in your life. I
pray that each day you count your blessings,
and rejoice in the Lord Jesus Christ our
Savior.

Amen

14064978R00026

Made in the USA
Charleston, SC
18 August 2012